THE CHIMPANZEE LADY
JANE GOODALL

BIOGRAPHY BOOK SERIES FOR KIDS
CHILDREN'S BIOGRAPHY BOOKS

DISSECTED LIVES
auto biographies

Speedy Publishing LLC

40 E. Main St. #1156

Newark, DE 19711

www.speedypublishing.com

Copyright 2017

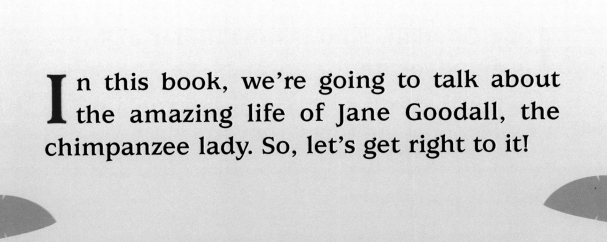

In this book, we're going to talk about the amazing life of Jane Goodall, the chimpanzee lady. So, let's get right to it!

WHO IS JANE GOODALL?

Jane Goodall, who is now in her eighties, is an advocate for animals. She's also an ethologist. As an animal rights advocate and activist, Jane believes that animals should never be killed in ways that cause them intense pain.

chimpanzee

As an ethologist, she has spent her life studying chimpanzees in their wild, natural habitats. Because chimps are primates and their DNA only differs from humans about 1.2%, her studies have also had a huge impact on anthropology.

Anthropology is the study of how humans behave in their societies and cultures. Jane is a respected scientist, author, and speaker who is known around the world for her work. During her lifetime she's received almost 50 honorary degrees.

EARLY LIFE

Jane was born in London in 1934 and from the start it seemed that she was destined to have a very exciting life. Her father owned businesses and loved to drive racecars. Her mother was an author who wrote novels under a pen name.

Jane grew up in a household where adventure, research, and writing all combined into passion for work and for life.

Bournemouth

Jane and her sister Judy spent their early childhood years in London and then in a city called Bournemouth, a seaside resort about 90 miles southwest of London.

Jane was only one year old when her father brought home a special toy for her birthday. It was a stuffed toy chimp. It was a replica of the real female chimp that had just been born at the London Zoo. The family named the toy chimp "Jubilee," because that year was the silver jubilee of King George V. It was Jane's first encounter with a chimp and no one realized how it would affect her future life!

From that moment on, Jane had a fascination with all types of animals, but especially African animals. When she got older, she meandered around the town of Bournemouth. She fancied herself as the field scientist she would someday become. She watched the native animals carefully and recorded their anatomy and behavior in her naturalist notebooks. She loved to read and she studied all the books she could get on zoology and animal behavior. In her dreams, she saw herself traveling to Africa where she could see elephants, giraffes, and chimpanzees in the wild.

A TRIP TO KENYA, AFRICA

Jane went to a private school and graduated when she was 18. She got a job at Oxford University and started to save money to make a trip to Africa. That's when she got her first big break. A friend of hers offered her a chance to visit Kenya.

Africa

Leakey

Once she was there she had an even more incredible piece of luck. Through some other friends, she met Louis Leakey. Leakey was a famous paleoanthropologist.

Leakey with wife Mary

Jane knew so much about natural history that she immediately impressed Leakey and he didn't hesitate.

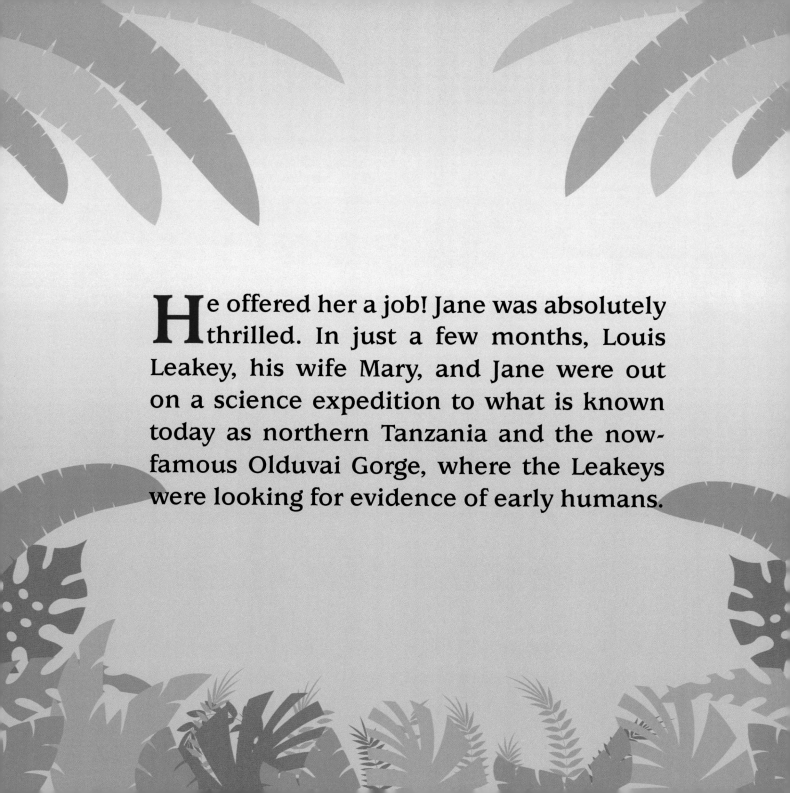

He offered her a job! Jane was absolutely thrilled. In just a few months, Louis Leakey, his wife Mary, and Jane were out on a science expedition to what is known today as northern Tanzania and the now-famous Olduvai Gorge, where the Leakeys were looking for evidence of early humans.

Olduvai Gorge

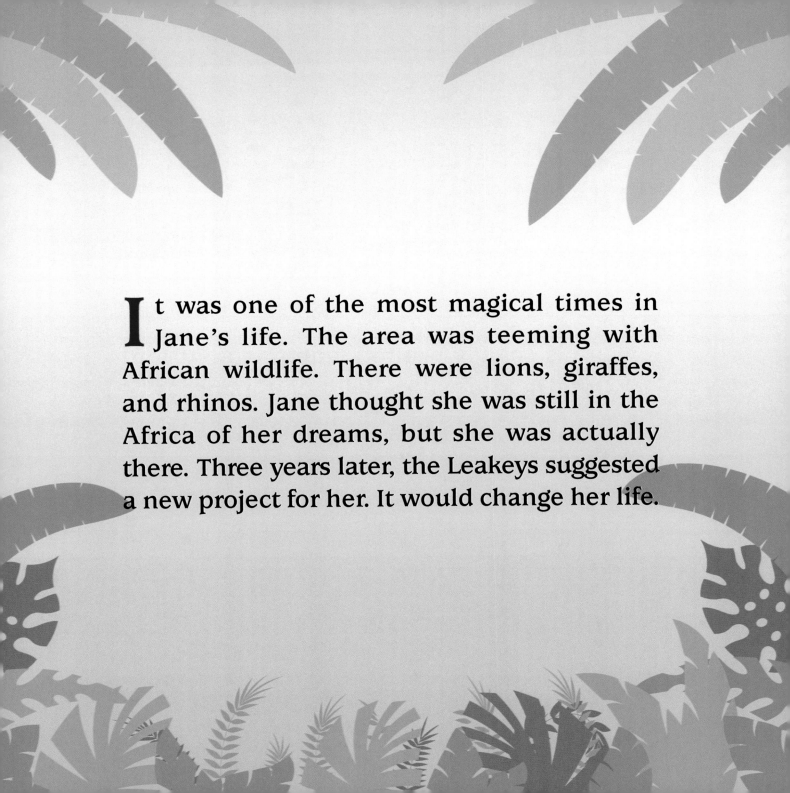

It was one of the most magical times in Jane's life. The area was teeming with African wildlife. There were lions, giraffes, and rhinos. Jane thought she was still in the Africa of her dreams, but she was actually there. Three years later, the Leakeys suggested a new project for her. It would change her life.

THE GOMBE STREAM CHIMPANZEE RESERVE

Louis Leakey wanted Jane to go out into the field to study wild chimpanzees at the Gombe Stream Chimpanzee Reserve, which was located at the edge of Lake Tanganyika. Only one other naturalist had ever tried to study chimps in their native habitat before.

CARE. CONSERVE AND PROTECT FOR FUTURE GENERATIONS

REGULATIONS.
IS PROHIBITED TO:
DISTURB ANY BIRDS OR ANIMALS.
FEED ANIMALS
LEAVE THE CAMP WITHOUT A PARK
GUIDE.
TAKE A CHILD BELOW THE AGE OF
5 YRS OLD INTO THE PARK.
CUT. OR DESTROY ANY PART OF
THE VEGETATION.
BRING A PET OR WEAPON INTO THE
PARK.

WHILE OBSERVING ANIMAL
IT IS PROHIBITED TO:
• GET CLOSER THAN 10M.
• CARRY FOOD.
• USE FLASH WHILE TAKING
  PHOTOGRAPHS.
• FRIGHTEN ANY INFANT BABOON
  CHIMPANZEE.
• STARE DIRECTLY INTO EYES OF
  ANIMALS.
• TALK LOUDLY, RUN OR CALL.
• MAKE SUDDEN MOVEMENT.
• PLAY WITH ANIMALS.

Entrance to Gombe Stream National Park

There had been a huge staff to help that naturalist, but Jane, one hired assistant, and Jane's mother ventured to the reserve. Jane wanted to go alone, but she wasn't allowed to do so.

Gombe Stream National Park, Tanzania

Jane was twenty-six years old and it was considered too dangerous for her to be there by herself.

With the help of a local game warden, Jane and her mother pitched a tent. It was warm and when they needed air they just opened up the flaps of the tent.

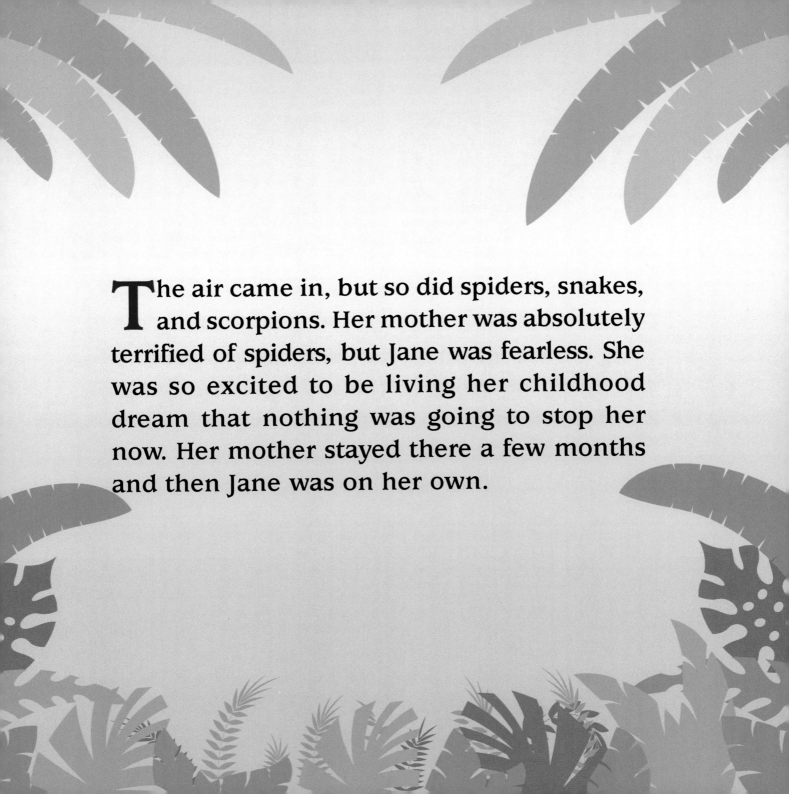

The air came in, but so did spiders, snakes, and scorpions. Her mother was absolutely terrified of spiders, but Jane was fearless. She was so excited to be living her childhood dream that nothing was going to stop her now. Her mother stayed there a few months and then Jane was on her own.

THE CHIMP CALLED DAVID GREYBEARD

At the beginning, Jane was having trouble getting close to the chimps. She tried different techniques to see if she could get closer to them. She witnessed that the chimps had different personalities and she gave them whimsical names. She named one of the chimps David Greybeard.

One day in October of 1960, she noticed that David Greybeard was doing something unusual. He was eating a small bush pig that he had killed.

J ane was very surprised because up until then naturalists had thought that chimpanzees were strict vegetarians.

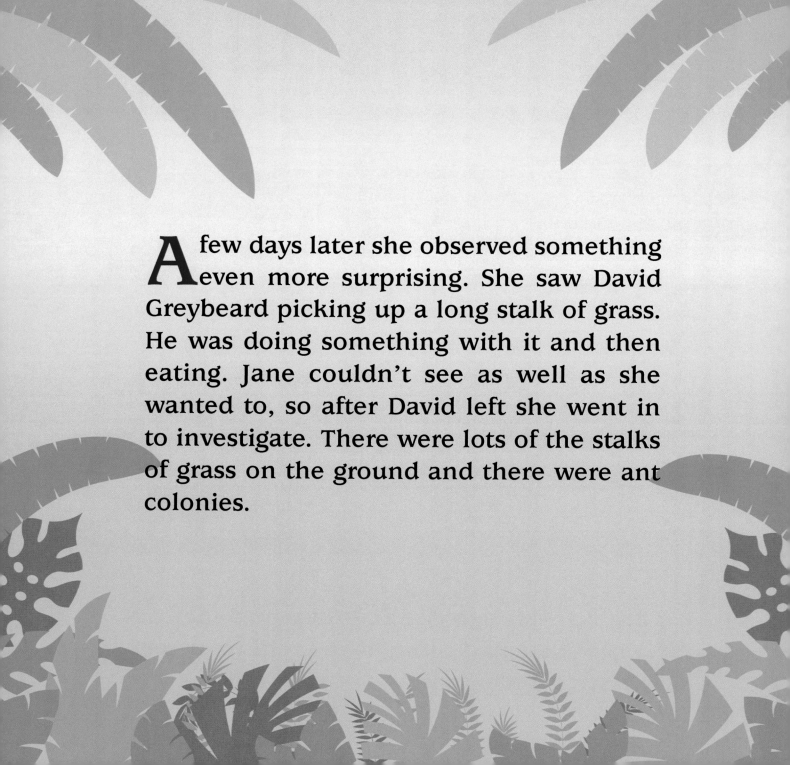

A few days later she observed something even more surprising. She saw David Greybeard picking up a long stalk of grass. He was doing something with it and then eating. Jane couldn't see as well as she wanted to, so after David left she went in to investigate. There were lots of the stalks of grass on the ground and there were ant colonies.

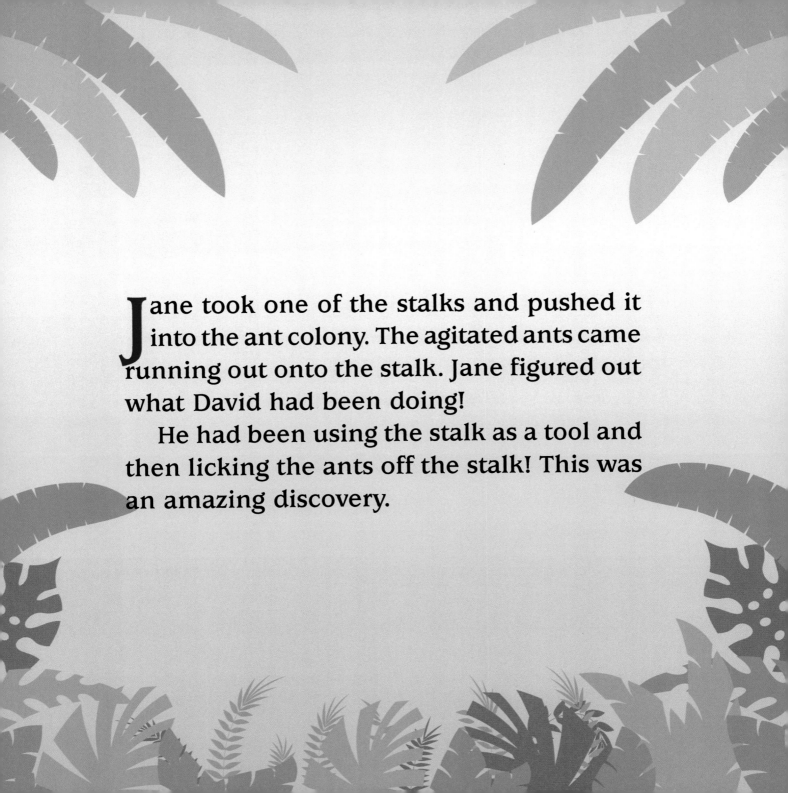

Jane took one of the stalks and pushed it into the ant colony. The agitated ants came running out onto the stalk. Jane figured out what David had been doing!

He had been using the stalk as a tool and then licking the ants off the stalk! This was an amazing discovery.

At that time, it was thought that only humans used tools to do things. She had to be sure, so she waited until she had witnessed the same behavior numerous times before telling Louis Leakey about it.

JANE GOES TO CAMBRIDGE

The Leakeys were very excited about Jane's findings. Louis helped Jane enroll in a program to get her doctorate at Cambridge. Jane really didn't want to do it. She just wanted to continue her work in the field. When Jane presented her findings to other scientists at Cambridge, instead of being interested, they ridiculed her.

Some of them thought that Jane had taught the chimps how to use the stalks and that they hadn't done it on their own. They made fun of the fact that she could recognize their personalities and had named them. Jane didn't let their criticism get to her. She knew in her heart they were wrong and she would prove it. Things got worse before they got better though. In April of 1962, she studied for hours to present her findings at the London Zoological Society.

Solly Zuckerman

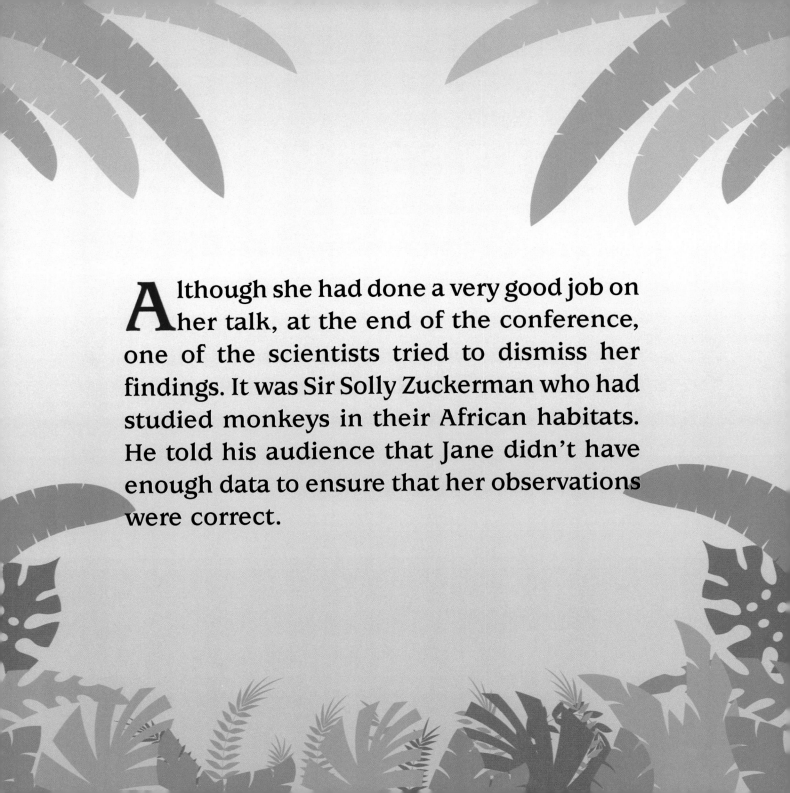

Although she had done a very good job on her talk, at the end of the conference, one of the scientists tried to dismiss her findings. It was Sir Solly Zuckerman who had studied monkeys in their African habitats. He told his audience that Jane didn't have enough data to ensure that her observations were correct.

THE CHIMPANZEES AT THE LONDON ZOO

Jane had had an opportunity to humiliate Zuckerman the year before and she had chosen not to do it. Jane was appalled at the conditions of the living space for the chimpanzees at the London Zoo. During the hot summer, their enclosure had no shade and it was unbearably hot for them. She was giving a press conference at the zoo at the end of 1961.

London Zoo

London Zoo

She was going to expose the conditions and request that the housing for the chimps be fixed. When he heard of her plan to talk about these poor conditions in a public conference, Jane's associate Malcolm MacDonald suggested that she would offend Zuckerman who was the head of the zoo and therefore create a potential enemy. She decided not to ridicule Zuckerman in public and worked with MacDonald to get some changes made in the chimps' living conditions. It was the beginning of her advocacy for chimpanzees, which she's continued through today.

JANE'S AMAZING FINDINGS

During Jane's twenty-five years living with the wild chimpanzees she made many amazing discoveries that changed the thinking of scientists all around the world. She found out that chimps have strong family bonds and a very complicated social system. She found out that they have a primitive language that has about 20 different sounds.

She discovered that they use hugs to comfort each other and have long-term relationships with their family members. They aren't vegetarians. It was surprising when she discovered that they eat meat and sometimes eat other chimps.

In 1986, at the age of 52, she went traveling to advocate for better treatment of chimpanzees around the world and she has continued her work through today.

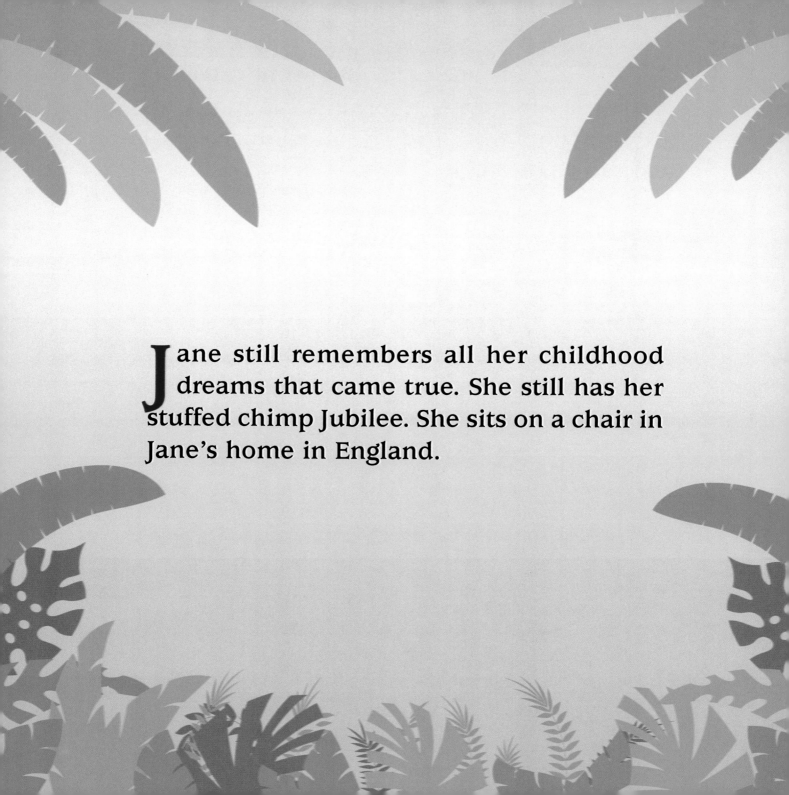

Jane still remembers all her childhood dreams that came true. She still has her stuffed chimp Jubilee. She sits on a chair in Jane's home in England.

SUMMARY

Jane Goodall has been an animal rights activist and ethologist her whole life. At a very early age she was fascinated by African animals and knew that she wanted to go to Africa to observe animals in the wild. Louis Leakey helped Jane and believed in her work. He gave her the opportunity to study chimpanzees in the wild. Jane lived with the chimps for over twenty-five years and made amazing discoveries that influence the way scientists view chimpanzees today.

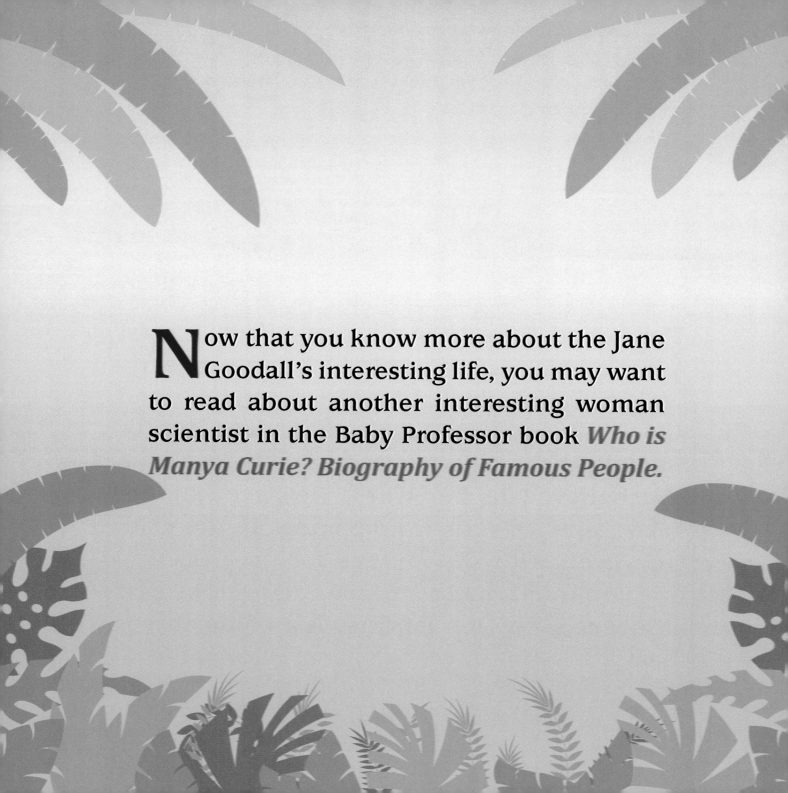

Now that you know more about the Jane Goodall's interesting life, you may want to read about another interesting woman scientist in the Baby Professor book *Who is Manya Curie? Biography of Famous People.*

Visit